The Ultimate Book of Balls

Volume 1

Sweet

By Susan Lehmkuhl

The Ultimate Book of Balls

Volume 1

Sweet

By Susan Lehmkuhl

Published by BBN Publishing
HOUSE
in the United States of America

BOOK DEDICATION

Dedicated to my health

FOREWORD

I've been challenged with weight issues all my life and, to add to that, I love sweets and carbs. Recently I moved in with my 91 year old mom to be her caretaker. She is thin and eats carbs, cookies, and ice cream as staples. In the first 3 months we lived together, I gained 20 pounds. I quickly realized that I couldn't keep it up so I started eating healthy again and since I did the cooking so did she. She didn't stop eating the sweets but she was getting more veggies and good proteins. After a couple of months of resisting any sweets, I got a craving and decided to see what I could find that wouldn't take me totally off-kilter. I found a recipe for energy balls and, as they say, the rest is history. I've had a blast mixing these up, trying new combinations, and sharing my balls with friends and family. I hope you enjoy them as much as I do.

TABLE OF CONTENTS

BALL Tricks, Tips, & Hints

If the dates or other dried fruit are dry or hard, let soak in hot water for 7-8 minutes, then drain and pat dry. Don't let them get soggy!

Dough consistency is similar to raw cookie dough.

Mix ingredients then cover and refrigerate for at least 30 minutes. This will make the dough less sticky and easier to work with.

Pulse just the dates in the food processor until they are in small pieces before adding remaining ingredients.

Balls can be rolled in a variety of different ingredients to add flavor, texture, and make them less messy.
Cinnamon Coconut Seeds Nut Cocoa

Cut up dates or other ingredients before putting into the food processor to avoid having as many chunk up incidents.

For those with nut allergies, try sunflower seeds or hemp hearts.

Store balls in an airtight container in the refrigerator for up to 10 days but they won't last that long!

Balls can be frozen for up to 2 months.

Frozen balls can be eaten immediately or let them sit a few minutes to warm up.

JOYFULLY ALMOND Balls

INGREDIENTS

1/2 cup all-natural crunchy almond butter
1 (8 oz) package pitted dates
2 tablespoons melted coconut oil
3/4 cup old fashioned oats
3/4 cup unsweetened flaked coconut
1 teaspoon vanilla extract
1/4 teaspoon almond extract
1/4 teaspoon salt

DRIZZLE

1/2 cup dark chocolate chips
1 teaspoon coconut oil

INSTRUCTIONS

Line a rimmed baking sheet with a silicone baking mat.
Combine almond butter, dates, 2 tablespoons melted coconut oil, oats, coconut, vanilla extract, almond extract,
and salt in food processor and combine until dough forms
then

SCOOP, ROLL, & DROP

Put in freezer for 30 minutes

Melt dark chocolate chips and coconut oil in microwave, then carefully drizzle each bite with chocolate.

PUMPKIN Balls

INGREDIENTS

8-12 pitted Medjool dates
1 cup oats1/4 cup pumpkin puree
1 tablespoon sugar free maple syrup
    plus additional 1-3 teaspoons as desired
1 tablespoon chia seeds or ground flaxseed meal
2 1/4 teaspoons pumpkin pie spice or swap:
    1 1/4 teaspoons ground cinnamon
    1/2 teaspoon ground ginger
    1/4 teaspoon ground nutmeg
    1/8 teaspoon cloves
1 teaspoon pure vanilla extract
1/8 teaspoon kosher salt
A dash of cayenne pepper to give it a kick (optional)

INSTRUCTIONS

Pulse just the dates in the food processor
until they are in small pieces and form a sticky ball.

Add remaining ingredients then

SCOOP, ROLL, & DROP

Peanut Butter Balls

INGREDIENTS

1 cup unsalted, natural creamy peanut butter
½ cup coconut flour
3 tablespoons low carb keto maple syrup

INSTRUCTIONS

Mix all ingredients together then

SCOOP, ROLL, & DROP !

HEMP SEED Balls

INGREDIENTS

1 cup oats, rolled or quick
½ cup hemp hearts
6 medjool dates, pitted and chopped
3 tablespoons sugar free maple syrup
½ teaspoon vanilla extract
½ teaspoon cinnamon, optional
pinch of salt, optional

INSTRUCTIONS

Pulse just the dates in the food processor
until they are in small pieces and form a sticky ball.

Add remaining ingredients then

SCOOP, ROLL, & DROP

If the dough is too dry, add a little water,
1 teaspoon at a time.

CAKE Balls

INGREDIENTS

1 cup all-natural drippy cashew butter*
1/3 cup + 1 tablespoon vanilla protein powder
1/2 cup rolled oats
1 tablespoon honey
1 teaspoon vanilla extract

INSTRUCTIONS

Mix all the ingredients in bowl, then

SCOOP, ROLL, & DROP

NOTES

You want drippy cashew butter. If it's too dry, the doubt will not hold form. Creamy peanut butter or almond butter can be used as a substitute.

MONSTER COOKIE Balls

INGREDIENTS

1 cup creamy peanut butter
1/4 cup sugar free pancake syrup
1 tsp vanilla extract
1 ¼ cups rolled oats
3 tablespoons chia seeds
¼ cup coconut
¼ cup pumpkin seeds
1/2 cup chocolate candies
¼ cup mini chocolate chips
1/4 tsp sea salt

INSTRUCTIONS

Combine all the ingredients to form a dough.
Let chill for 15-20 minutes then

SCOOP, ROLL, & DROP…

Sprinkle a little flaky sea salt on top of the
bites and enjoy!

SPICY DATE BALLS

INGREDIENTS

1 cup unsalted cashews
15-18 dates, pitted
2 tbsp cocoa powder
1/4 tsp mild chili powder
1 tsp cinnamon
tiny pinch cayenne pepper
1 tsp pure vanilla extract

INSTRUCTIONS

Grind down nuts. Add remaining ingredients mixing until it forms a dough then

A little cayenne goes a long way so use sparingly

SCOOP, ROLL, & DROP

Roll them in some toasted coconut for added flavor

SALTED CHOCOLATE Balls

INGREDIENTS

1¼ cups pitted dates
1 cup walnuts
3 tbsp cocoa powder
2 tbsp coconut oil, melted
1 tsp vanilla extract
1 tbsp sugar-free pancake syrup
½ tsp cinnamon
¼ tsp cayenne
2 oz dark chocolate (about 70% cocoa), chopped
¼ tsp flakey salt

INSTRUCTIONS

Grind walnuts in a food processor container.
Add dates,
cocoa powder, coconut oil, vanilla, maple syrup or honey,
cinnamon and cayenne and blend until dough forms.

SCOOP, ROLL, & DROP!

Microwave chocolate in a small bowl on high in 20-second
intervals until melted, stirring between each interval.
Drizzle chocolate over balls and sprinkle with salt.

Chill for about 30-40 minutes then eat!

OATMEAL RAISIN Balls

INGREDIENTS

1 cup rolled oats
½ cup steel cut oats
¼ cup ground flax seed
1 cup raisins
1 tsp cinnamon
dash nutmeg
dash salt
2 tsp vanilla
1½ Tbsp sugar-free pancake syrup
½ cup almond butter

INSTRUCTIONS

Add dry ingredients into a bowl and mix. Add the remaining ingredients and mix to form a sticky dough, then

SCOOP, ROLL, & DROP

If the dough is too sticky, add more rolled oats. If the dough is a bit too dry, add more almond butter to get just the right consistency.

CHOCOLATE CHIP BALLS

INGREDIENTS

1 cup raw almonds
½ cup old fashioned oats
¼ cup almond or peanut butter
7 – 8 medjool dates, pitted and chopped
1 teaspoon vanilla
2 tablespoons water, + plus more as needed
⅓ – ½ cup dark mini chocolate chips or cacao nibs

INSTRUCTIONS

Grind down almonds and oat to make a flour.
Add remaining ingredients, except chips, and combine until dough forms. Add 1 or 2 tablespoons more water as needed.

Add chocolate chips by hand and chill for about 20 minutes then:

SCOOP, ROLL, & DROP!

Balls can be rolled in cacao powder, cinnamon, or coconut for added texture and flavor.

GINGER COOKIE Balls

INGREDIENTS

1 cup rolled oats
3/4 cup almond butter
1/2 cup finely shredded unsweetened coconut
1/2 cup ground flaxseed meal
1/4 cup sesame seeds
1/4 cup sugar free pancake syrup
1 teaspoon ground cinnamon
1/2 teaspoon ground ginger
1/4 teaspoon ground cloves
1/4 teaspoon sea salt

INSTRUCTIONS

Mix all your ingredients together until dough forms. Place the bowl in the refrigerator for 10 minutes, then

SCOOP, ROLL, & DROP

FLIRTY SPICE Balls

INGREDIENTS

Energy Balls
1 1/4 cups gluten-free rolled oats
1 TBS espresso powder
(+/- depending on preference)
1 tsp ground cinnamon
1/2 tsp cardamom
1/4 tsp ground ginger
1/8 tsp all spice
1/8 ground cloves
1/8 tsp ground nutmeg
1 TBS chia seeds
1/2 cup creamy natural nut or seed butter
1/3 cup honey
1/2 tsp vanilla extract
2 TBS cacao nibs (or mini chocolate chips)

INSTRUCTIONS

Combine all your ingredients and mix well.

Once the dough is formed place in the freezer for about 10 minutes then

SCOOP, ROLL, & DROP

PB&J Balls

INGREDIENTS

2/3 cup creamy peanut butter
1/3 cup sugar-free pancake syrup
1 1/4 cups rolled oats
1/2 cup mixed dried blueberries or strawberries
2 TBSP chia seeds
2 TBSP hemp hearts (optional)

INSTRUCTIONS

Combine ingredients together to form a sticky dough. Place bowl in freezer for about 10 minutes then

SCOOP, ROLL, & DROP

BROWNIE Balls

INGREDIENTS

1/2 cup walnuts
1/2 cup almonds
1 cup dates Medjool, chopped
1/3 cup + 2 teaspoons unsweetened cocoa powder
1/2 cup shredded coconut flakes
pinch salt

INSTRUCTIONS

Grind the walnuts and almonds in a food processor to create fine meal. Add the dates, cocoa powder, ¼ cup shredded coconut flakes and salt.
Mix until dough forms then

SCOOP, ROLL, & DROP!

Roll in remaining coconut for taste and texture

CHAI SPICE Balls

INGREDIENTS

1 1/2 cups raw cashews
1/2 teaspoon KOSHER SALT
1 teaspoon cinnamon
1/2 teaspoon ground ginger
1/4 teaspoon cardamom
2 cups packed, pitted medjool dates

INSTRUCTIONS

Put cashews and spices into a food processor mix to fine meal. Add dates and then

SCOOP, ROLL, & DROP!

Enjoy!

CINNAMON Balls

INGREDIENTS

1 ½ cups raw almond
1 1/3 cups unsweetened finely shredded coconut
1 cup fresh dates, pitted
3 tbsp honey
1 ½ tsp ground cinnamon or to taste

For the frosting:
2 tbsp coconut butter, melted
2 tsp honey

INSTRUCTIONS

Put almonds in a food processor and chop until fine. Add shredded coconut, pitted dates, honey and cinnamon and process until you get a dough.

Chill the dough in the refrigerator for 30 minutes then

SCOOP, ROLL, & DROP!

Icing is optional

FIG ALMOND Balls

INGREDIENTS

15 dried Mission figs
7 pitted Mejool dates
1/4 cup natural almond butter
3/4 cup oats
1/4 cup ground flaxseed meal
1 teaspoon pure vanilla extract

INSTRUCTIONS

Place all of the ingredients food processor pulse for 2-3 minutes until the mixture forms nice dough then

SCOOP, ROLL, & DROP!

DARK CHIP Balls

INGREDIENTS

1 cup almond flour
2 tbsp honey
3 tbsp natural creamy cashew nut butter
1 tbsp unsweetened almond milk
2 tbsp mini dark chocolate chips

INSTRUCTIONS

Combine all ingredients EXCEPT chips in the food processor adding milk slowly until dough forms. Fold in chips by hand. the almond flour, honey, cashew butter and process to combine.

Cover and chill the dough in the refrigerator for 30 minutes.then

SCOOP, ROLL, & DROP

CASHEW BUTTER Balls

INGREDIENTS

½ cup raw almonds
½ cup toasted hazelnuts
½ cup natural creamy cashew nut butter
4 tbsp honey
1 tsp pure vanilla extract

INSTRUCTIONS

Grind almonds and hazelnuts until finely chopped. Add the cashew nut butter, honey, and pure vanilla extract and mix until you get a dough Cover and chill the dough in the refrigerator for 30 minutes then

SCOOP, ROLL, & DROP

CANDYBAR BALLS

INGREDIENTS

1/2 cup cashews
1/4 cup oats
2 tablespoons creamy peanut butter
2 tablespoons dark chocolate chips
1 tablespoon sugar free maple syrup
1/2 tablespoon chia seeds
1/2 teaspoon vanilla extract

INSTRUCTIONS

Put all the ingredients into food processor and combine until dough is formed, then

SCOOP, ROLL, & DROP

PEANUT BUTTER OATMEAL Balls

INGREDIENTS

1 cup oats
⅔ cup toasted shredded coconut
½ cup peanut butter
½ cup mini chocolate chips
⅓ cup honey
1 Tbsp. chia seeds
1 tsp vanilla

INSTRUCTIONS

Combine all ingredients in a large bowl then

SCOOP, ROLL, & DROP

PROTEIN Balls

INGREDIENTS

1/2 cup almond butter or peanut butter
1/2 cup vanilla protein powder
1/3 cup coconut flour or oat flour*
plus 1-2 tablespoons additional as needed
1 1/2 sugar free pancake syrup
1 teaspoon pure vanilla extract
1/4 teaspoon cinnamon
2-4 tablespoons unsweetened vanilla almond milk
or milk of choice or water
2 tablespoons dark chocolate chips

INSTRUCTIONS

Mix ingredients together to create dough.
Add additional coconut flour if too sticky or
more almond milk if too dry then

SCOOP, ROLL, & DROP

SHORTBREAD Balls

INGREDIENTS

1 1/2 cups almond flour
8 pitted dates
1/4 cup vanilla protein powder
1/2 teaspoon vanilla extract
pinch of salt
2 tablespoons of water

Coating:

1/4 cup almond flour
2 tablespoons vanilla protein powder

INSTRUCTIONS

Combine all ingredients, except for coating Ingredients, in a food processor and blend on high until dough forms then

SCOOP, ROLL, & DROP.

Roll balls in the coating mixture

SUNFLOWER Balls

INGREDIENTS

½ cup old fashioned rolled oats
1 Tablespoon flaxseed
1 Tablespoon chia seeds or hemp seeds
2 Tablespoons raisins (optional)
2 Tablespoons chocolate chips
pinch of sea salt
½ cup sunflower seed butter
1 Tablespoon sugar-free pancake syrup

INSTRUCTIONS

Mix all ingredients together to form dough then

SCOOP, ROLL, & DROP

About The Author

Susan Lehmkuhl is an eclectic author who found her voice during the Covid pandemic.

She currently lives in Sun City, AZ where she is blessed with being the full-time caretaker for her 91-year-old mother.

Susan writes not only recipes (and yes, she tries them all), she also writes poetry, self-help books, and romance.

Check out all her books on Amazon

Follow Susan on Social Media

Like WHICHSUSAN on FACEBOOK

Follow WHICHSUSAN on INSTAGRAM

Other Books by the Author

POETRY

Fire from ICE
Transitions
Seduction

PEACE OF MIND PLANNERS

GYM BUDDY

RECIPES

Ultimate Book of Balls
Volume 1
Volume 2
Volume 3
Volume 4

Review the Book

Dear Readers:

It means the world to me that you read my book and try the recipes. Your feedback is really important to me. I'd like to ask a small favor. Would you be kind enough to leave an HONEST review on Amazon?

Thank you so much!

I'd also like to invite you to join my mailing list. I don't send out a lot of newsletters but when I do they're full of good stuff like poetry, free recipes and more. Just head over to my website to sign up. SUSANLEHMKUHL.com

Until we meet again,

Susan Lehmkuhl

Made in the USA
Monee, IL
12 December 2023